Golden Reflections

A Dog's Tale

Written by Carolee Nance Kolve
Illustrated by Susan Anderson-Shorter

AuthorHouse™
1663 Liberty Drive
Bloomington, IN 47403
www.authorhouse.com
Phone: 1-800-839-8640

© 2010 Carolee Nance Kolve. All rights reserved.

No part of this book may be reproduced, stored in a retrieval system, or transmitted by any means without the written permission of the author.

First published by AuthorHouse 2/17/2010

ISBN: 978-1-4490-4641-5 (sc)

Library of Congress Control Number: 2010901537

Printed in the United States of America
Bloomington, Indiana

This book is printed on acid-free paper.

authorHOUSE®

For Lady, of course,
and the people who loved her best.

Mama just hated that rude word for girl dogs, and she told her daughters, quite firmly, that we needed to be ladies. "You are to be cheery little angels," she said, "and above all, never complain."

So it's been my policy to keep a positive attitude, but I must tell you that typing is no picnic for a dog. Our paws were made for important work (like digging!), and this keyboard could use a major new design for the canine customer. But on the plus side, I get to sit on my mother's favorite chair and reflect on a life of love, good deeds, and just enough mischief to be interesting. When a girl makes it to one hundred in dog years, it's time to tell her story.

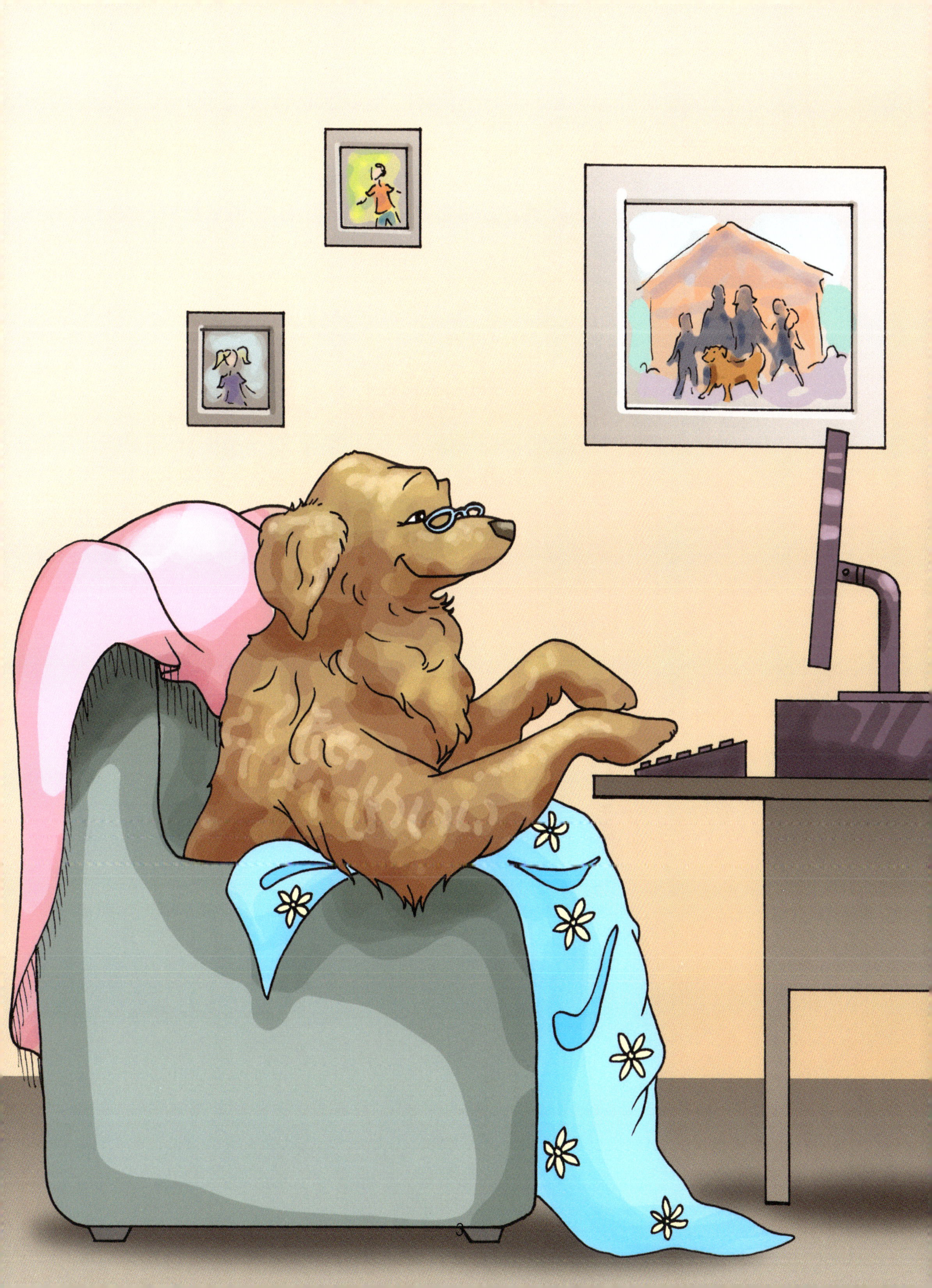

I was born to fine parents in the sweet-smelling, wet state of Oregon. We were of the extra-fluffy, reddish-gold branch of the golden retriever family. Mama would scold me for bragging, but people do say that when the summer sunlight strikes our coats we are the most beautiful dogs on earth … but I digress.

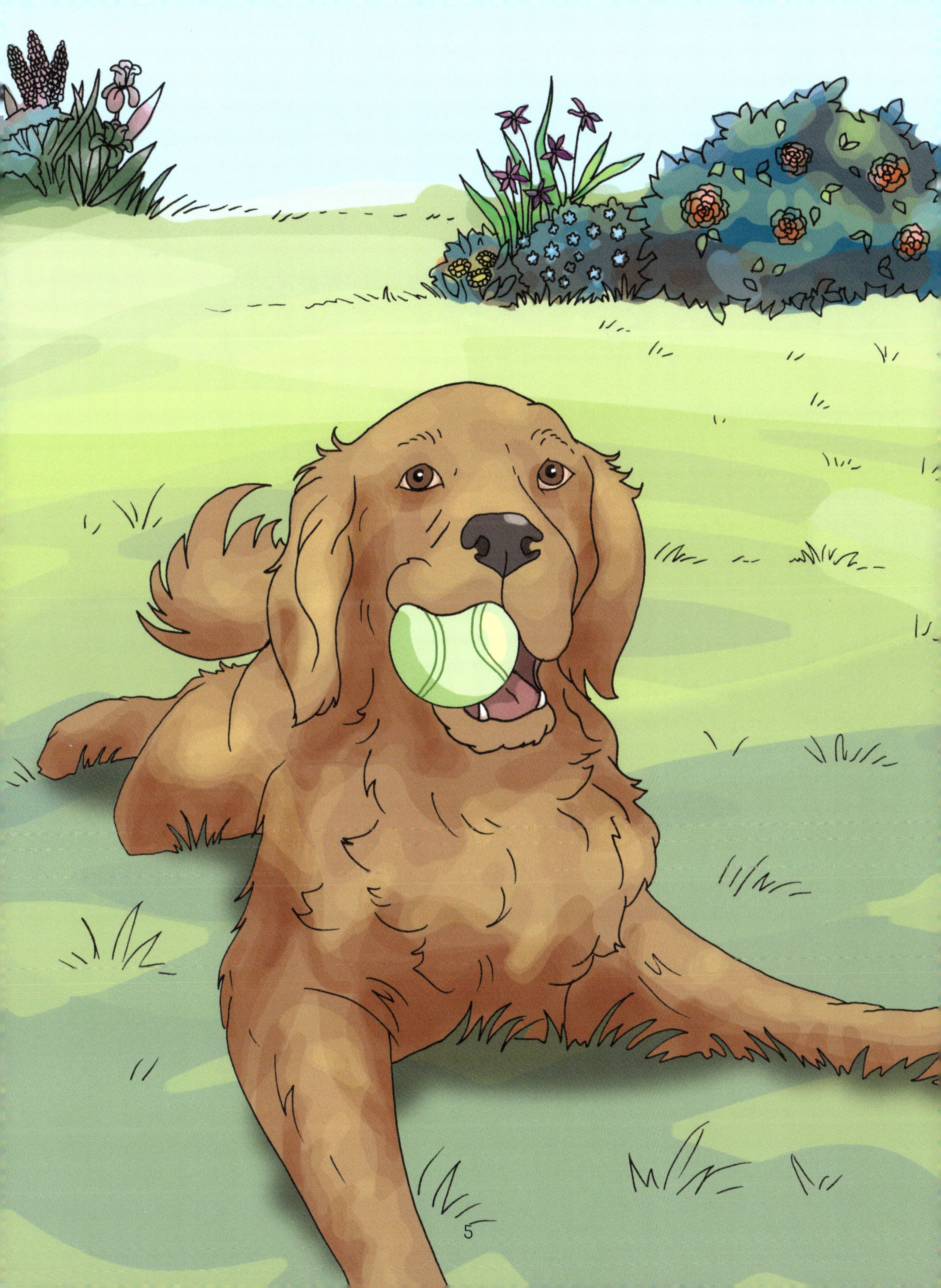

My mother was a lovely and elegant creature, but with Papa living in a different house, and twelve puppies to raise, she soon grew haggard. After only a few weeks, she was ready to be rid of us all. "I'm sorry, children," she said. "I love you each, but I can no longer cope. You must find new homes."

Scads of families came to smooch and squeeze us, but I only remember the first. Mama nudged us all out of our box and onto the floor, where we were expected to make a good impression.

"Wag those tails!" she cried.

My sisters and I pranced and sniffed with a friendly-but-dignified wag, but our brothers were such show-offs! Lurching and twirling, tumbling and chewing, bumping and burping—it was so embarrassing.

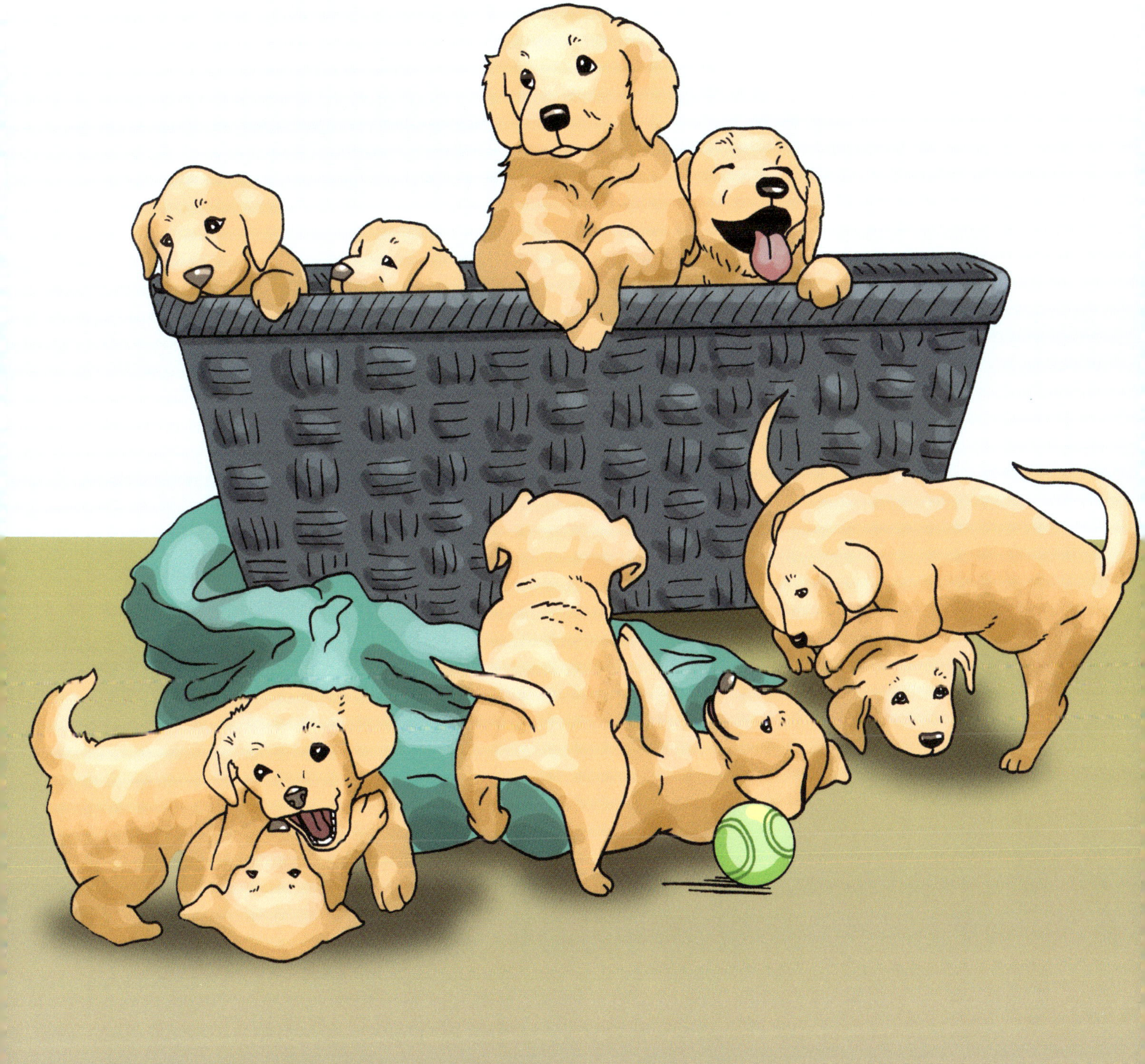

I looked at this family and knew instantly that I liked the little boy. He was about six years old, and he was watching me in the nicest way. My heart started thumping like crazy, and I went over and washed his feet. He picked me up gently and said, "This is the one I want." Then I licked his face and he hugged me. My birth owner put a black K on my ear and said the Kolves could come get me in two weeks.

I couldn't believe I was the first puppy picked! Mama said it was because I was such a good girl. My brother said, "No, it's because she's a slobbertylick." So I tiptoed over and drooled in his ear!

At last my new family came to take me home. As we left, I could hear Mama calling, "Obey your new mother! Lick everyone you meet! Be a pleaser! Always remember, you are a golden retriever!" (Like I didn't know this stuff already!)

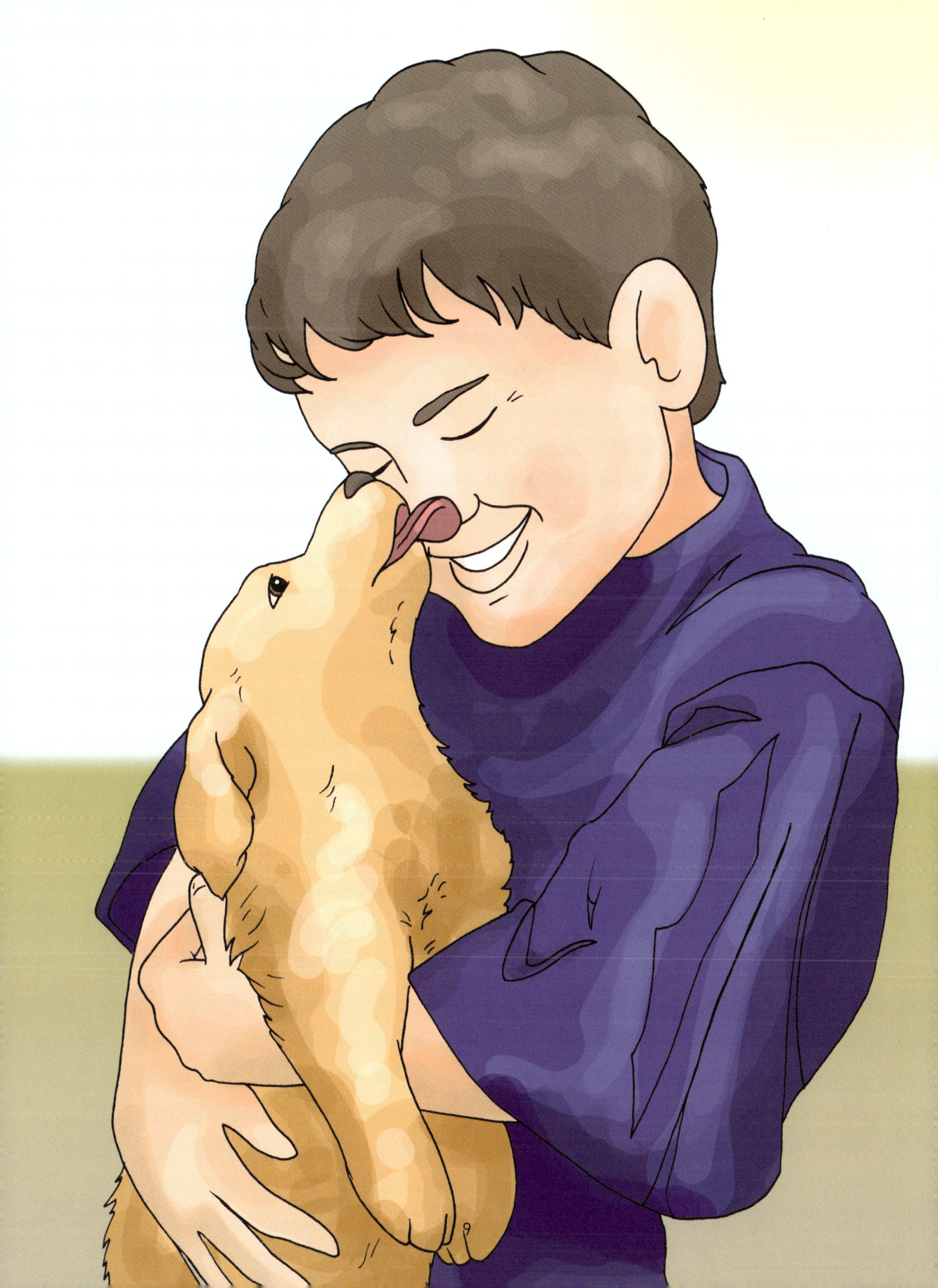

In the car I learned my new brother was Kris and that we had a sister named Lindsay, a same-house dad, and a stay-at-home mom. Then they told me that I was an only dog and that my name was to be Lady—can you believe it?—Lady! I loved my new family so much—they kept petting and kissing me, and I couldn't lick them enough!

Kris was my special pal. At quiet times, we would cuddle and hug, and sometimes I licked away his troubles. Then we would play like maniacs! We played with tennis balls, towels, pillows, and toys, but my favorite game was stealing his underwear. (Dirty socks were good, too!)

I slept in his room every night; sometimes he got in my bed, and sometimes I got in his!

11

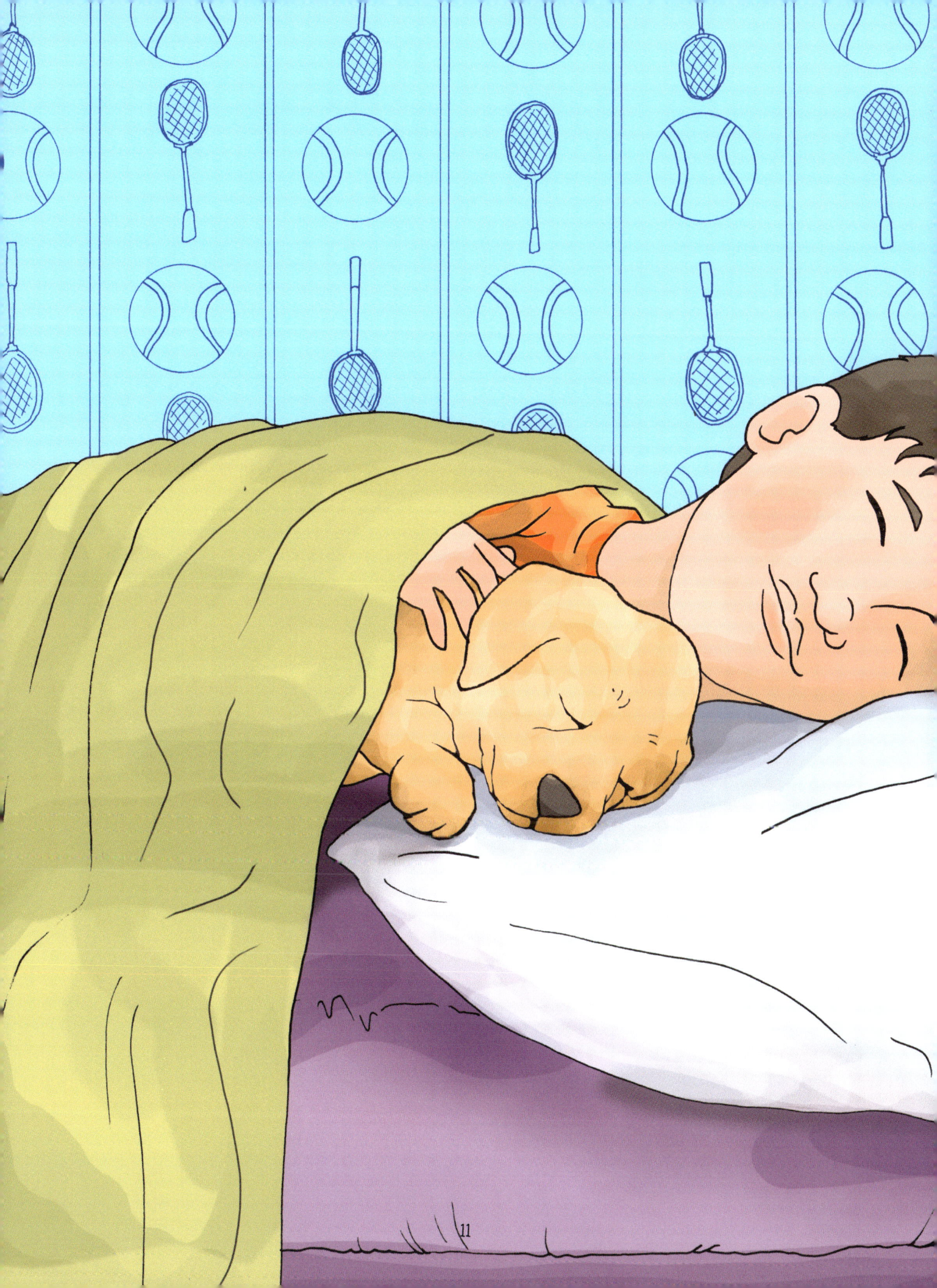

Lindsay was the best tummy-scratcher and the gentlest petter, and she never forgot to feed me when Mom and Dad went to a party. At dinner I always tried to be under her chair so she could sneak me her vegetables. I would have rather had her meat, but veggies are better than nothing. Except for onions. Yuck! I hid those under the rug.

Mom was my main feeder and trainer. She never got tired of taking care of me. (Of course, she didn't have eleven other children like poor Mama.) She taught me perfect manners: "Lady, Sit. Down. Stay. Shake. Come." I loved minding my mother and usually got a treat or at least a "Good dog!" Except when she said, "Lady, off the couch."

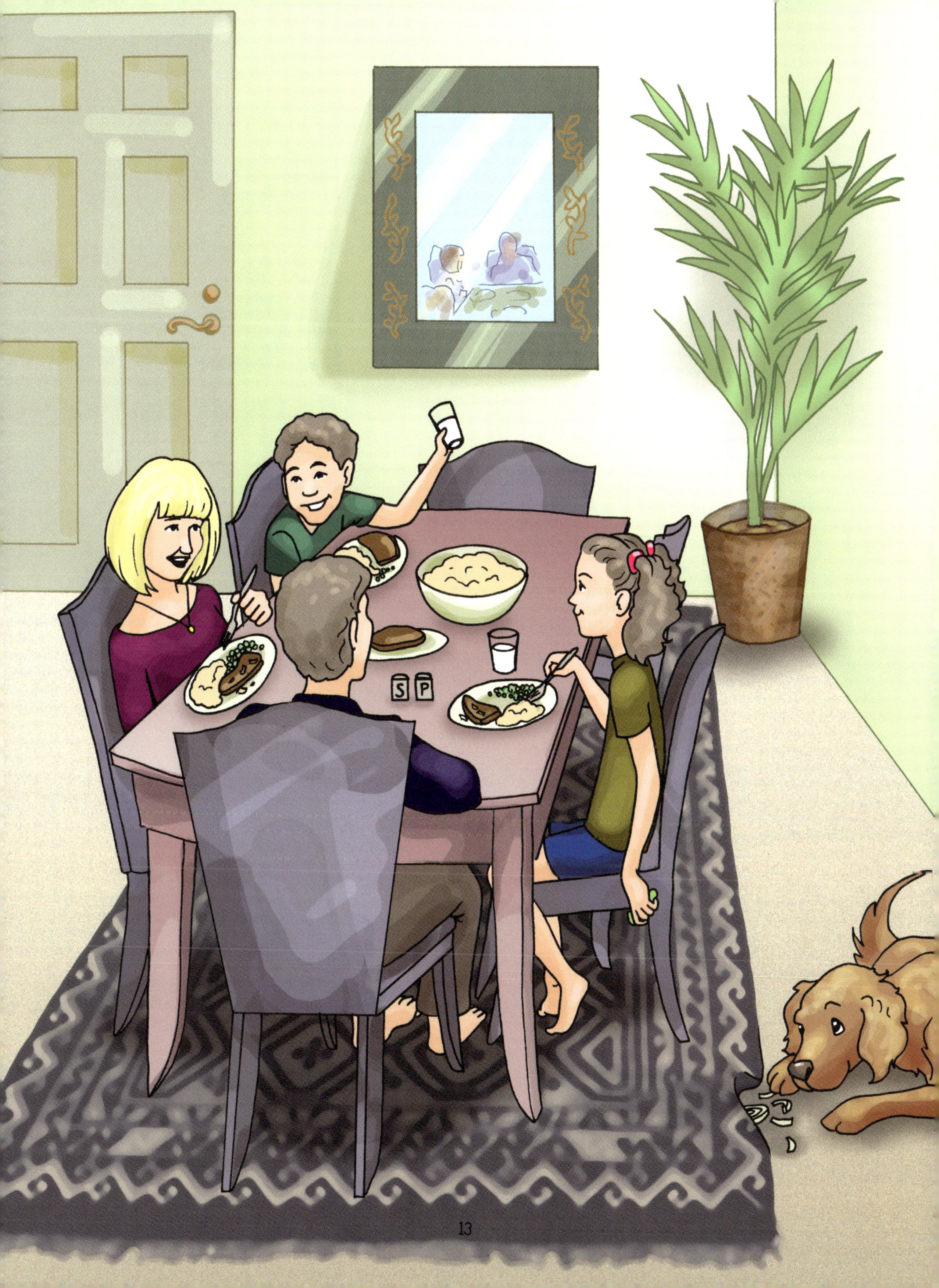
S
P

Dad had the finest arm in the family and would throw tennis balls way into the woods for me to retrieve. He loved to do this for guests and bragged, "You won't believe how fast she is!" Of course, after years of playing this game, there were thousands of balls in the woods, so I just grabbed the first one I saw and zoomed back to my cheering audience. It made Dad so happy, and would you believe that neither he nor his friends could ever smell the difference?

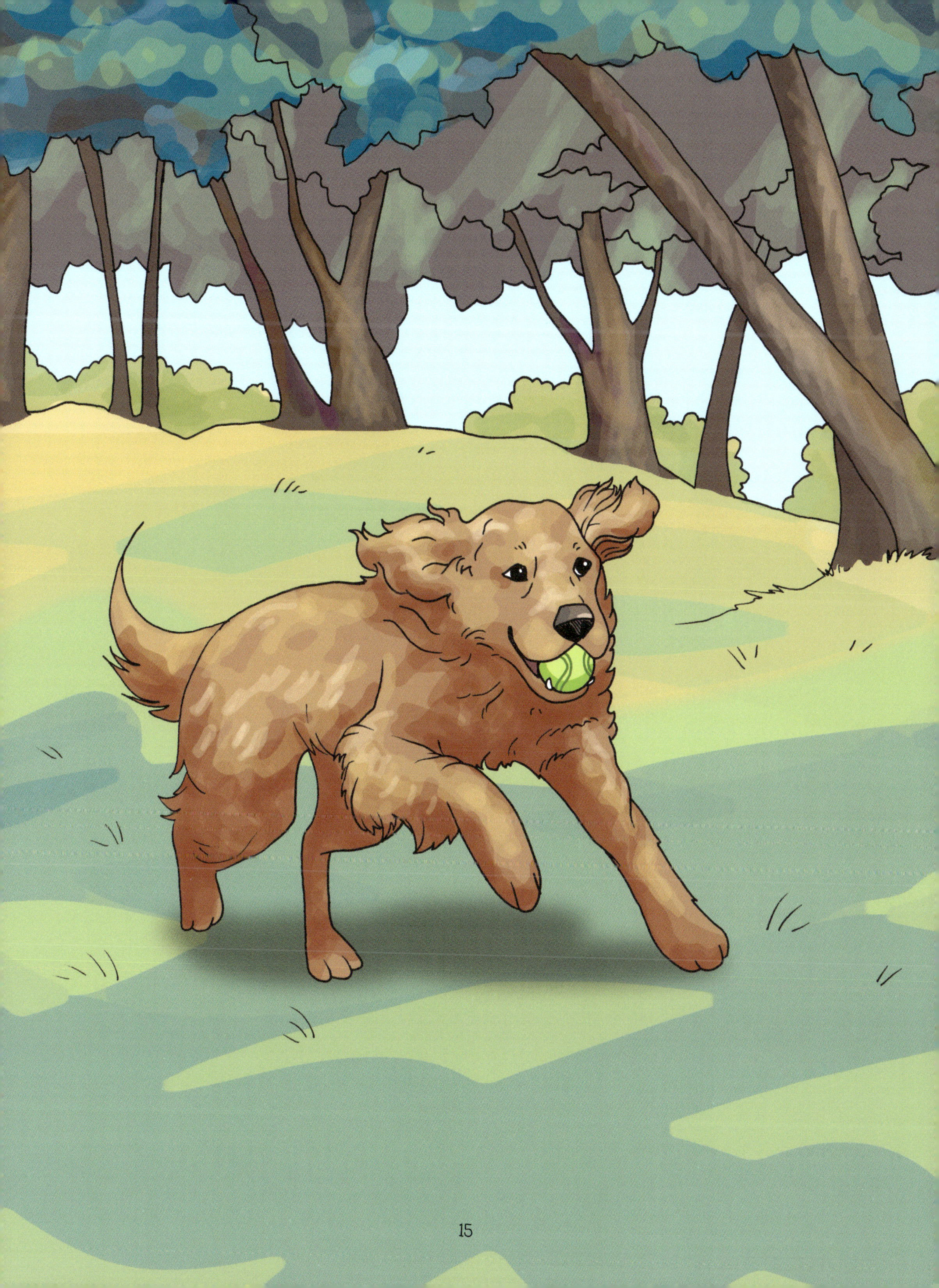

Kris and Lindsay grew and grew, and they had lots of friends who came to the house to play with me. But sometimes I got the feeling I wasn't the center of their lives anymore, especially when they said, "Lady, down and stay." I tried hard to get their attention. I crept over and nuzzled their legs. I bumped my nose under their hands so they would pat me. And sometimes I just jumped on their laps and gave them a big, soggy lick right on the mouth!

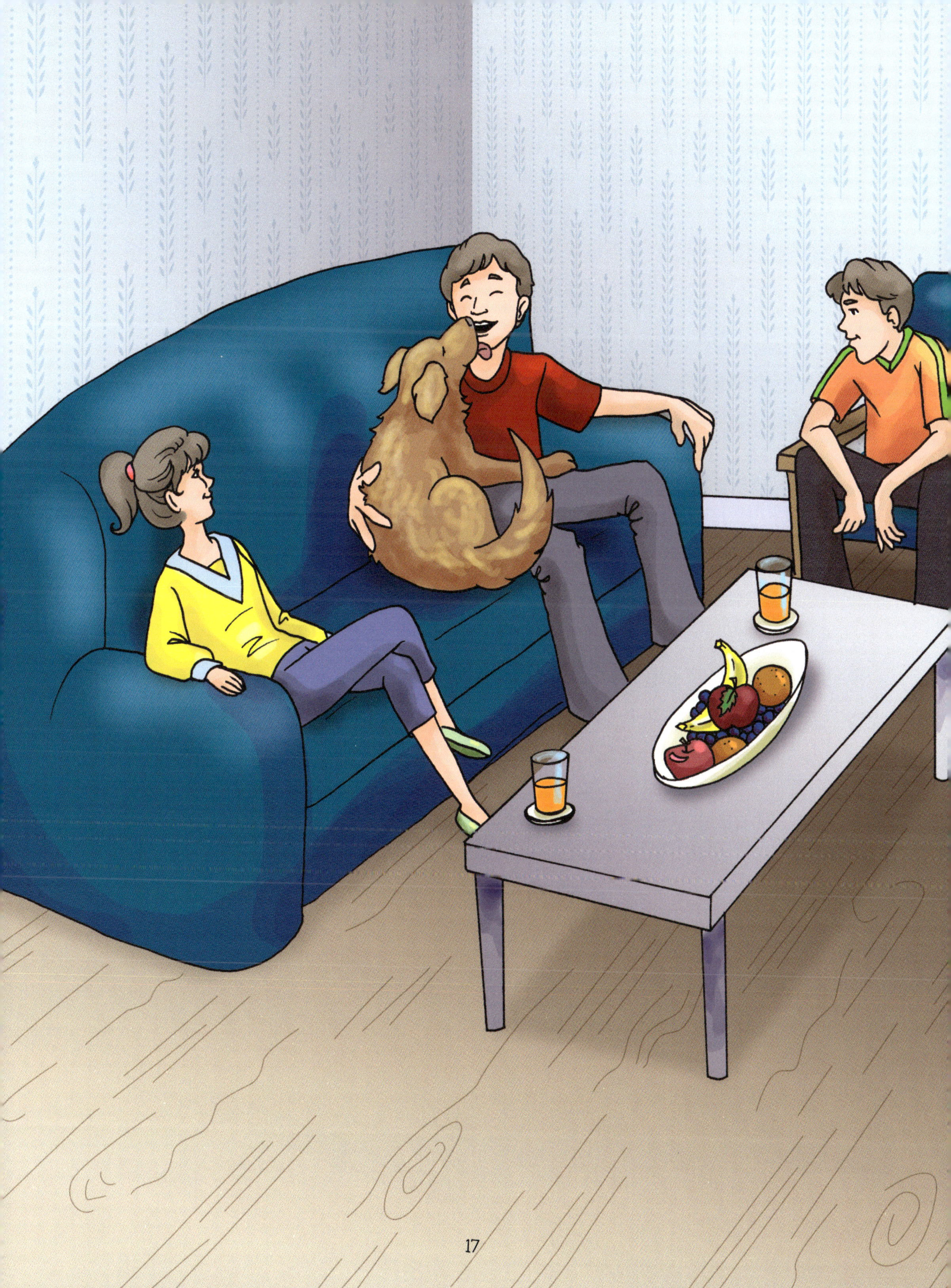

About once a year my family went on a trip without me. Believe me, nothing will spoil a dog's day like the sight of a suitcase and the words "We'll be home soon, Lady." And those infernal evenings out! I quivered and danced every time they came home—but when they were gone? I had issues. I had boredom! I had to pass the time somehow.

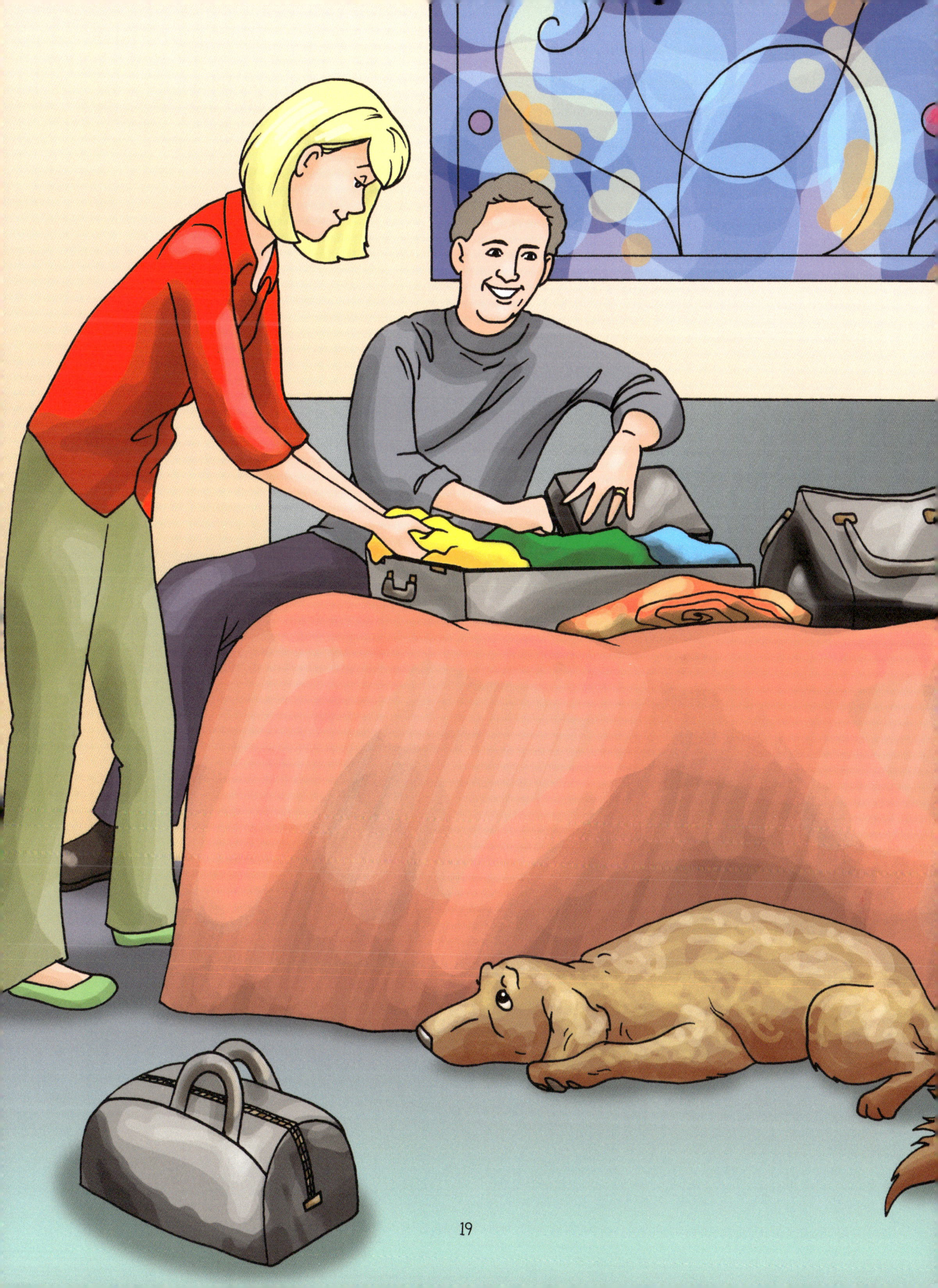

I tried consoling myself with food. First, I licked the butter dish on the kitchen counter. But they scolded me and hid the butter. Once, I ate all the Halloween candy. But then they took me to the vet, who made me throw up everything, even the wrappers. I gobbled up meat that was defrosting, cookies that were cooling, and bananas that were getting ripe in the window. My favorite score was a wheel of brie cheese in puff pastry which Mom put on that nice, low table in the living room. Delicious! But after that she put me outside when food was around.

21

Next, I decided to pass the time alone with important work. I thought about digging holes. I thought about pulling up flowers. I considered chewing the patio furniture. I thought about all my tennis balls in the woods. Then I hit upon the perfect project—finding my balls and burying them in secret places! Don't ask me why this was so much fun. It just was.

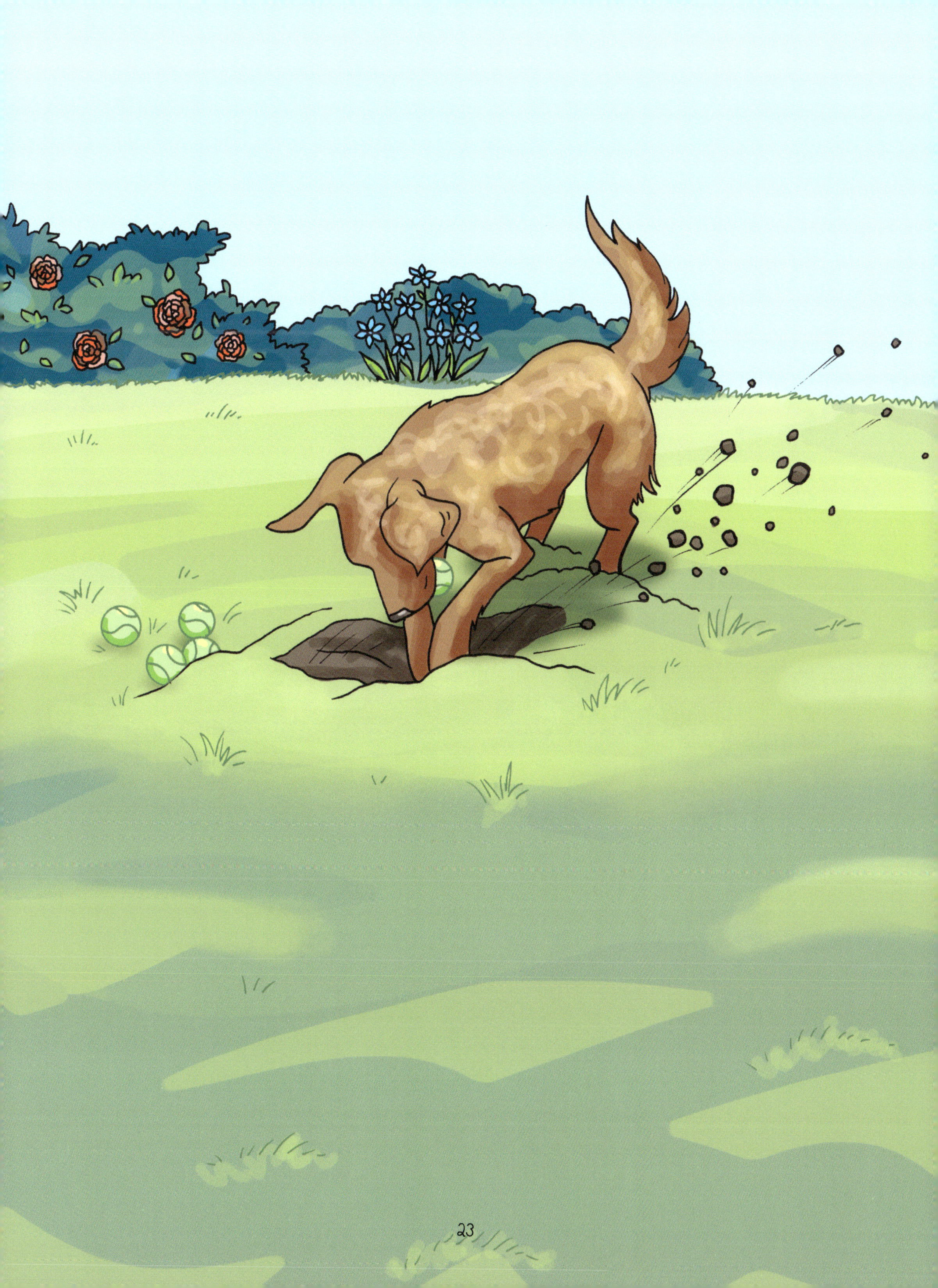

Then one day, Lindsay left to go to college, and pretty soon, Kris went to college, too. They said they couldn't take me with them, so I was thinking, How great can this college place be if they don't allow dogs? I was lonesome when they left.

I moped outside their bedroom doors. Food helped a little, and burying more balls helped a little. I even tried hiding balls in the house. But I was still sad.

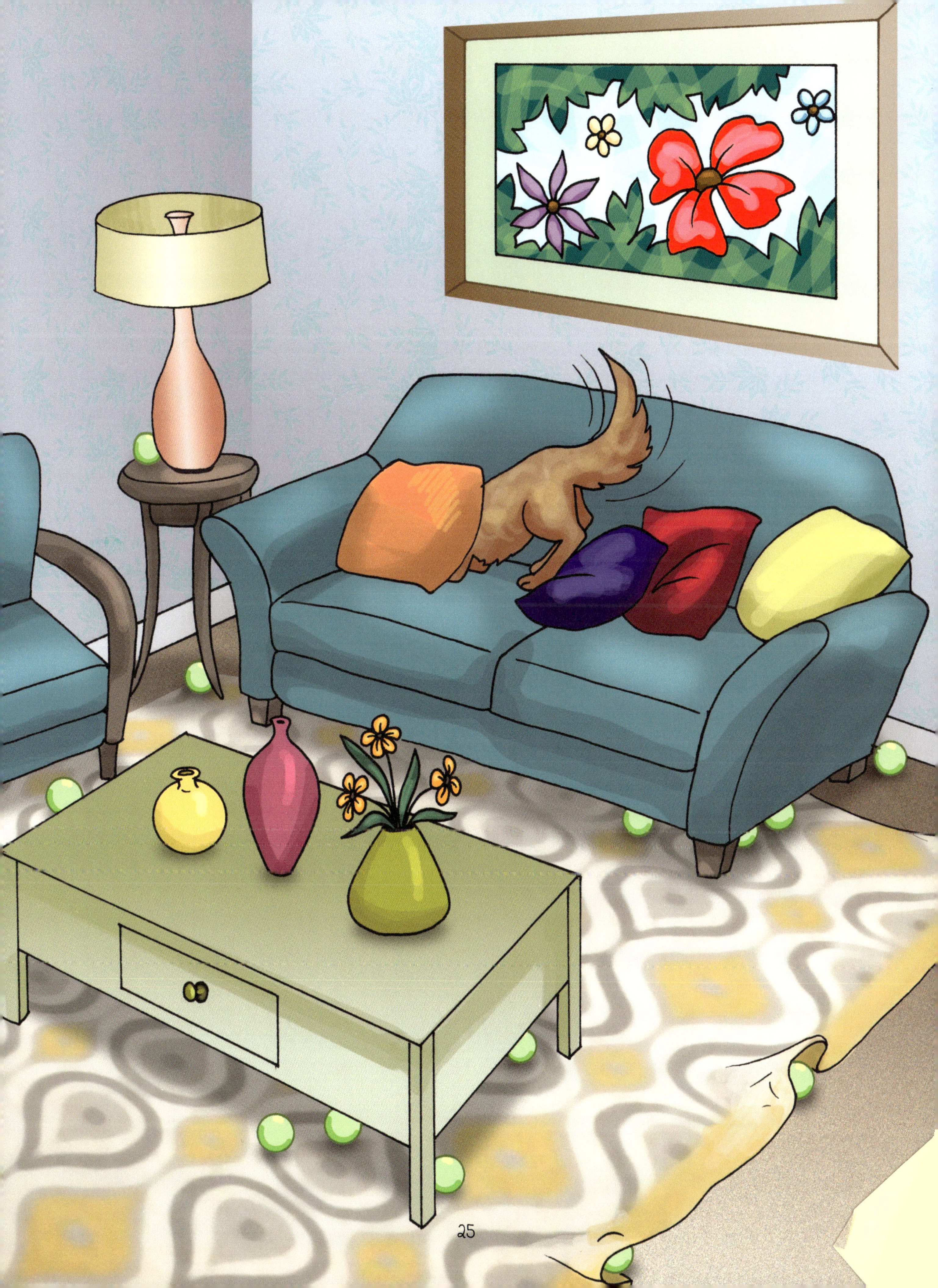

Mom was sad too, but she hugged me and said, "Lady, our buddies left the nest, but we have each other." She started taking me on long walks and could almost keep up with me! (I was never big on heeling.) And she took me everywhere in the car with the windows rolled down. I loved the feel of the breeze blowing and the heavenly smells of other dogs' poop all around town! But everywhere we went, I thought about my buddies.

Looking back, I've had a love-packed, mostly healthy life. I've survived rat poisoning, epilepsy, back surgery, and knee surgery, and I tried my best to beat kidney failure. When Kris and Lindsay left for college, it was my hardest time. I had to learn to stay busy and hold them patiently in my heart.

Now they are home for Christmas, and for the first time, I'm the one going off without them. I can see in their eyes that they don't want me to go. I lick their hands gently, and I can feel their love and their sadness. But they'll be happy again soon after I'm gone. Because you see, I've learned that once we love someone, they never really leave us. In your mind and your heart, where it matters most, they are always with you.

If ever you miss me, you can glance out the window at my favorite spot on the lawn. And when you look with your heart, you'll see me there, on the grass, with a tennis ball in my mouth and the summer sunlight glowing on my hair.

And when you find the balls I've hidden for you,
I know you'll even smile.